THE BEST CUSTOMER SERVICE QUOTES EVER SAID

JOHN R. DIJULIUS III

RIVER GROVE
BOOKS

Published by River Grove Books
Austin, TX
www.rivergrovebooks.com

Copyright ©2016 John R. DiJulius III

All rights reserved.

No part of this book may be reproduced, stored in a retrieval system, or transmitted by any means, electronic, mechanical, photocopying, recording, or otherwise, without written permission from the copyright holder.

Distributed by River Grove Books

For permission to reprint copyrighted material, grateful permission is given to the following sources (credits continued on page 118, which serves as an extension of the copyright page):

Zeke Adkins: From "Customers Are Not Always Right. They Are Just Never Wrong" by Zeke Adkins from *Entrepreneur*. February 19, 2015, accessed February 16, 2016 at www.entrepreneur.com/article/243004.

AMACOM via Copyright Clearance Center: From *Delivering Knock Your Socks off Service* by Kristin Anderson and Ron Zemke, Third Edition. Copyright © 1998.

Design and composition by Greenleaf Book Group and Debbie Berne
Cover design by Greenleaf Book Group and Debbie Berne

Cataloging-in-Publication data is available.

Print ISBN: 978-1-63299-087-7

First Edition

Previous books by John R. DiJulius III

*Secret Service: Hidden Systems That Deliver
Unforgettable Customer Service* (Amacom, 2003)

*What's the Secret? To Providing a World-Class
Customer Experience* (Wiley, 2008)

*The Customer Service Revolution: Overthrow
Conventional Business, Inspire Employees, and
Change the World* (Greenleaf, 2015)

DEDICATION

I live by the quote "Surround yourself with great people and hopefully you will be guilty by association." My greatest strength is who I surround myself with in both my professional and personal lives. This book is dedicated to my amazing team at The DiJulius Group, especially Denise Thompson, Nicole Paul, David Wagner, Mary Iacobucci, Dave Murray, and Claudia Medica. All of your hard work, loyalty, and genuine passion for what you do make me look good. Each of you execute so many things flawlessly, allowing me to do what I do best—write, speak, consult, read, research, and create new content. You deserve so much more credit than you receive. I cannot thank each of you enough for your faith in my vision and the way you live The DiJulius Group's purpose—*To Change the World by Creating a Customer Service Revolution*.

INTRODUCTION

Welcome to *The BEST Customer Service Quotes Ever Said* journal. I love quotes. I am enamored with quotes. Quotes inspire me and make me think. I have been creating and collecting quotes on customer service and customer experience for over twenty years. This book is a collection of the best quotes ever said on the subject of customer service and customer experience.

I didn't want it to be just a quote book that sits on a desk and collects dust. This is why I combined it with a journal. I want people to be able to use this daily at work and in meetings, to carry it around to write down notes and thoughts, and to use the quotes to inspire them and their teams to build world-class customer service organizations. I want them to be inspired to be part of the customer service revolution, to make price irrelevant, and to be the brands customers cannot live without.

I hope you enjoy these quotes as much as I do. Now let's go make some history—stuff that people will talk about for decades to come, that may end up in the history books, and redefines the way things are currently being done.

QUOTES

Here are some suggestions for how you can use *The BEST Customer Service Quotes Ever Said*:

- Share one quote every day with your team and have them think and share how they can make that apply to their role with their customers and your organization.

- Have your employees each select a quote they like and say why they think it is so important.

- Send out a quote of the day via email to your employees.

- Include a different quote daily or weekly at the bottom of your email signature.

- Include a quote on customer invoices.

1. "[We are at our] best when creating enduring relationships and personal connections . . . When we are fully engaged, we connect with, laugh with, and uplift the lives of our customers—even if it is just for a few moments . . . It's really about human connection."
—**Howard Schultz**

2. "You do not merely want to be considered just the best of the best. You want to be considered the only one who does what you do."
—**Unknown**

3. "Let's go make some history today—stuff they will talk about for decades to come, that may end up being written about in books, redefining the way things are currently being done."
—**Unknown**

4. "Serving others is the meaning of why we are alive, not what we do when it is convenient or can come back to benefit ourselves."
—John R. DiJulius III

5. "Don't compete in price wars, compete in experience wars."
—John R. DiJulius III

6. "A customer is the most important visitor on our premises. He is not dependent on us. We are dependent on him. He is not an interruption in our work; he is the purpose of it. We are not doing him a favor by serving him. He is doing us a favor by giving us the opportunity to serve him."
—Unknown

7. "There's only one boss, the customer, and he can fire everybody in the company from the chairman on down, simply by spending his money somewhere else."
—Sam Walton

8. "Converting a service into an experience is when you take a mundane transaction and make it a unique, memorable moment."
—John R. DiJulius III

9. "A brand experience is the sum of experiential interactions your customers have that leave a lasting impression."
—John R. DiJulius III

10. "Experiential interactions are unique and memorable moments."
—John R. DiJulius III

11.
"The best way to greet someone is with the expression, 'There you are!'"

UNKNOWN

12. "Price is irrelevant when your customers are so happy with you, they have no idea what your competition charges."
—John R. DiJulius III

13. "Many times, when customers complain about price, it isn't because they are cheap or not willing to pay; it is because the experience didn't justify it."
—John R. DiJulius III

14. "Outlove your competition."
—Seth Godin

15. "If you are able to figure out how to be truly interested in someone you meet, with the goal of building up a friendship instead of trying to get something out of that person, the funny thing is that almost always, something happens later down the line that ends up benefiting either your business or yourself personally."
—Tony Hsieh

16. "Stop trying to 'network' in the traditional business sense, and instead just try to build up the number and depth of your friendships, where the friendship itself is its own reward."
—Tony Hsieh

17. "Customer experience is where process meets design and art. It is about creativity and innovation in a system that allows you to build unique and memorable moments."
—John R. DiJulius III

18. "You have to be an artist to build an incredible customer experience."
—John R. DiJulius III

19. "The purpose of a business is to create a customer who creates customers."
—Unknown

20. "Kindness is not an act—rather a lifestyle."
—Unknown

21. "I believe in a price match guarantee: if you find it higher somewhere else, we will raise our prices and experience to match it."
—John R. DiJulius III

22. "It is not your employees' responsibility to have high service aptitude; it is the company's to give it to them."
—John R. DiJulius III

23. "Are your customers a coupon away from going elsewhere?"
—Unknown

24. "Customer service is what you do; customer experience is how you do it."
—James Gilmore

25. "All a customer wants is someone who is nice to them, remembers them, and who is genuinely grateful to serve them."
—Unknown

26. "There is always someone who can make something a little crappier and sell a little cheaper."
—John R. DiJulius III

27. "Go beyond merely communicating to 'connecting' with people."
—Jerry Bruckner

28.

"Give whatever you are doing and whoever you are with the gift of your attention."

JIM ROHN

29. "Everybody around you has an invisible sign on their head which says, 'Make me feel important.'"
—Eric Philip Cowell

30. "If you're happy, tell your face!"
—Philip Hesketh

31. "Do not ask the customers what they want; give them something they cannot live without."
—Unknown

32. "The answer's yes. What's the question?"
—Cameron Mitchell

33. "An experience epiphany fills a gap customers didn't know they had and now cannot live without."
—John R. DiJulius III

34. "Give more than people expect, don't keep score, don't wait for them to do what they say, just do what you promised and a little more. If you borrow someone's truck or car, give it back to them with more gas and cleaner than they gave it to you."
—John R. DiJulius III

35. "Loyal customers are a different breed. They don't just come back, they don't simply recommend you, they insist that their friends do business with you."
—Chip Bell

36. "Build your company's customer experience as if no customer has bad intentions."
—John R. DiJulius III

37. "Always give without remembering; always receive without forgetting."
—Unknown

38. "Life is relationships; the rest is just details."
—Gary Smalley

39.

"Customer engagement
is a contact sport."

UNKNOWN

40. "I believe that we're starting something that is bigger than any of us can truly understand right now."
—Richard Branson

41. "Future generations will have it better as a result of what we are doing today."
—John R. DiJulius III

42. "For all the promise of digital media to bring people together, I still believe that the most sincere, lasting powers of human connection come from looking directly into someone else's eyes, with no screen in between."
—Howard Schultz

43. "You have to create an emotional experience that's so sticky, so engaging, so compelling that they don't want to leave. To compete in a tough market, you have to make your customers feel something."
—James Archer

44. "Your mission should be to have your client not be able to fathom how they could get along without you."
—John R. DiJulius III

45. "Be the brand customers cannot live without."
—John R. DiJulius III

46. "URX—you are the experience."
—John R. DiJulius III

47. "Lives will be changed for the better because we made a difference in someone's life at a time when they were just about to give up."
—John R. DiJulius III

48. "Yes, we better know our customers' names, but if you really delivered a great experience, the customer remembers our name."
—Ara Bagdasarian

49. "Be the best part of your customer's day."
—John R. DiJulius III

50. "Be the best decision your customers make."
—John R. DiJulius III

51. "Carpe momento—seize the moment! Our focus must be on providing a positive experience on EVERY interaction, whether it is face-to-face, click-to-click, or ear-to-ear."
—John R. DiJulius III

52. "An addictive experience happens when what you are providing is so extraordinarily unique and memorable your customers crave it, and it compels them to need again."
—John R. DiJulius III

53. "Demonstrate that no one cares about your client's business like you do."
—John R. DiJulius III

54. "A customer service revolution is a radical overthrow of conventional business mentality, designed to transform what customers and employees experience. This shift produces a culture that permeates into people's personal lives, at home, and in the community, which provides the business with higher sales, morale, and brand loyalty, thus making price irrelevant."
—John R. DiJulius III

55.
"Our clients want either the best or the least expensive."

TOM FIELD

56. "Eliminate the word *no* from your company's vocabulary; no employee should ever be allowed to use that word. You may not always be able to say *yes*, but offer alternatives and never allow anyone from your company to utter the word *no*. You will be amazed at how creative your team will get at satisfying customers."
—John R. DiJulius III

57. "... Customers are not always right; however, they're just never wrong."
—Zeke Adkins

58. "Don't concentrate on making a lot of money, but rather on becoming the type of person people want to do business with."
—Arthur Henry Fripp

59. "Elegance without warmth is arrogance."
—Horst Schulze

60. "Underpromise and overdeliver."
—Tom Peters

61. "It takes months to find a customer, seconds to lose one."
—Unknown

62. "A complaining client is giving us the opportunity to make things right; it's the silent ones that hurt us."
—John R. DiJulius III

63.

"Teach yourself to just say *yes*."

JOHN R. DIJULIUS III

64. "While you may feel like your client is demanding, your competition won't."
—John R. DiJulius III

65. "Creating raving team members will create raving customers."
—John R. DiJulius III

66. "The client is paying for their experience—not yours. Leave yours at the door."
—John R. DiJulius III

67. "Losing one customer may not affect sales, but all the potential customers they speak to will."
—John R. DiJulius III

68. "The ringing phone is next week's paycheck."
—John R. DiJulius III

69. "Nobody cares how much you know until they know how much you care."
—Theodore Roosevelt

70. "When advertising hype sets the bar too high, you can only disappoint."
—John R. DiJulius III

71. "Real customer service should be called custom service."
—Unknown

72. "The experience is remembered long after the price is forgotten."
—John R. DiJulius III

73. "The best way to regain a lost client is to not lose them in the first place."
—John R. DiJulius III

74. "The better the experience, the less price becomes an issue."
—John R. DiJulius III

75. "We do not lose any customers to a competitor we wouldn't lose anyway."
—John R. DiJulius III

76. "A complaint is like a consultant giving us vital information for free."
—John R. DiJulius III

77. "If you take really good care of your existing clients, they will generate more new customers than any kind of advertising campaign ever could."
—John R. DiJulius III

78. "The most selfless acts are the most rewarding."
—Unknown

79. "If you started over and took everyone's clientele away from them, within one year, the ones with the most clients would have the most again and the ones who didn't, wouldn't."
—John R. DiJulius III

80. "It's better to lose the money by being understaffed than to lose the reputation by serving the customer with just any employee."
—John R. DiJulius III

81.

"Service customers
like your company's life
depends on it."

JOHN R. DIJULIUS III

82. "It takes twenty years to build a reputation
and five minutes to ruin it."
—Warren Buffett

83. "Trust is about relationships. I will trust you
if I believe that you're in this for the long haul,
that you're not just trying to maximize your own
short-term benefits."
—David Maister

84. "When a problem arises with a customer, it gives us the opportunity to own the customer for life."
—Unknown

85. "The easiest customer to get is the one you already have."
—Norm Brodsky

86. "People don't remember what you said as much as how you made them feel."
—Unknown

87. "We are in the customer perception business."
—Mark Perreault

88. "Have an attitude for gratitude."
—Unknown

89. "Treat all customers as if your business revolves around them."
—John R. DiJulius III

90. "You are indispensable to your customer if you are the first person they call for anything, even the things you don't provide them."
—John R. DiJulius III

91. "One Profits Most Who Serves Best."
—Rotary International

92. "A sale is something that happens while you are immersed in helping to serve your customer."
—Unknown

93.

"No unhappy customer left behind."

JOHN R. DIJULIUS III

94. "Annual customer service training is like deodorant—pretty soon it wears off and the smell comes back."
—Unknown

95. "You've got to start with the customer experience and work backwards for the technology. You can't start with the technology and try to figure out where you're going to try to sell it."
—Steve Jobs

96. "The only businesses surviving with long-term sustainability are the ones fanatical about differentiating themselves through the customer experience they deliver."
—John R. DiJulius III

97. "Show me you care more about my business than just getting my business."
—Unknown

98. "In most cases our most recently hired, least-trained, lowest-paid employee deals with our customers the most."
—Unknown

99. "Don't win the argument but lose the customer."
—Unknown

100. "Your company is either creating brand evangelists or brand terrorists doing brand assassination."
—John R. DiJulius III

101. "Companies spend millions creating and advertising their brands, yet the customer's experience is what drives customer perception."
—John R. DiJulius III

102. "If you want to see how a company is doing now, look at their current sales; if you want to know how a company will perform in the future, look at their current customer satisfaction scores."
—Joe Calloway

103. "Many times the cheaper a customer goes, the more it ends up costing them."
—John R. DiJulius III

104. "If you are not serving the customer directly, you better be serving someone who is."
—Unknown

105. "You can say what you want about who you are, but people believe what they experience."
—Jack Mackey

106. "Secret Service is the ability to collect customer intelligence and utilize that to personalize their experience and get them to say, 'How'd they do that, and, How'd they know that?'"
—John R. DiJulius III

107. "Service aptitude is a person's ability to recognize opportunities to exceed a customer's expectations, regardless of the circumstances."
—John R. DiJulius III

108. "Ask the customer to describe the most memorable thing that took place during their last transaction with you."
—Jeffrey Gitomer

109.

"Is your company part of the customer service crisis or customer service revolution?"

JOHN R. DIJULIUS III

110. "Secret Service creates an emotional bond between customer and company that transcends the product or service."
—John R. DiJulius III

111. "Secret Service is not something you do; it is something that is in you. It is something that is in all areas of your life: your customers, employees, family, and neighbors."
—Brian Shelton

112. "We want our standards to be what our competition considers above and beyond."
—John R. DiJulius III

113. "Customer loyalty is won or lost at the front lines."
—John R. DiJulius III

114. "If you own the problem, you own the customer. If you lose the problem, you lose the customer."
—Robin Crow

115. "Focus on what you can do, not what you can't."
—Unknown

116. "People only crave what they have previously experienced and enjoyed."
—John R. DiJulius III

117. "Only focusing on first impressions can leave a bad taste in your customer's mouth."
—John R. DiJulius III

118. "While they may complain about the service defect, they are going to rave about how we handled it."
—John R. DiJulius III

119. "Nonnegotiable service standards make us a nonnegotiable part of our customers' lives."
—John R. DiJulius III

120.

"Build the experience and
the customers will come."

JOHN R. DIJULIUS III

121. "Innovation occurs when someone is
obsessively passionate about a particular
subject . . . that [improves] the human condition.
The people who obsess over these ideas cannot
imagine doing anything else. Thinking about
the idea consumes them, energizes them, and
ultimately inspires them to create breakthrough
companies, products, and services."
—Carmine Gallo

122. "When you truly serve people, your goal is not to make money or to get them to do what you want, but to take care of their needs and desires."
—Unknown

123. "When your customer talks, you sell. When you talk, you lose."
—Michael Dalton Johnson

124. "Your customer is whoever benefits from the work you do—or, conversely, whoever suffers when your work is done poorly or not at all."
—Ron Zemke

125. "Leaders serve those who serve others."
—Unknown

126. "Don't punish 100% of your customers for what you are afraid 2% might try to do."
—John R. DiJulius III

127. "Service is the desire to put the interest of others before ours."
—Unknown

128. "Your customers will never be any happier than your employees are."
—John R. DiJulius III

129. "We are here to enhance the quality of lives around us."
—John R. DiJulius III

130. "You can build the most beautiful space; however, it is your people who create the experience that keeps people coming back."
—John R. DiJulius III

131. "It is not your client and prospect's job to remember you. It is your responsibility to make sure they do not have the chance to forget you."
—Patricia Fripp

132. "A customer challenge is an opportunity to be a hero."
—John R. DiJulius III

133. "It is not the employer who pays the wages. Employers only handle the money. It is the customer who pays the wages."
—Unknown

134. "Rule #1—The customer is always right; Rule #2—If the customer is ever wrong, reread Rule #1."
—Stew Leonard's company's principle

135. "The only sustainable competitive advantage is a world-class customer experience. It cannot be copied or replicated. It cannot be outsourced or done overseas."
—John R. DiJulius III

136. "The most important component of a world-class experience is that the staff isn't focused on selling stuff. It's focused on building relationships and trying to make people's lives better."
—John R. DiJulius III

137. "Hire for attitude, not aptitude."
—Unknown

138. "It is better to reach your customers' hearts than their wallets. If you can touch your customers' hearts, profits will follow."
—Ron Johnson

139.

"Price is something
you offer when you have
nothing else."

UNKNOWN

140. "Life is like a game of tennis. The person who serves the best, wins."
—Ronald F. Arndt

141. "We see our customers as invited guests to a party, and we are the hosts. It's our job every day to make every important aspect of the customer experience a little bit better."
—Jeff Bezos

142. "You can have everything in life you want, if you will just help enough other people get what they want."
—Zig Ziglar

143. "The two most important words in a service recovery mindset are *compassion* and *empathy*."
—John R. DiJulius III

144. "Unhappy customers rarely say anything to you."
—John R. DiJulius III

145. "The goal of an excellent service organization is to deliver outstanding results with average employees."
—John R. DiJulius III

146. "When given the choice of obsessing over competitors or obsessing over customers, we always obsess over customers."
—Jeff Bezos

147. "Why do so many companies' agreements, policies, and signage sound so angry? You should be friendly to your customers at every touch point."
—John R. DiJulius III

148. "It's so much more powerful to aim for the smallest possible audience, not the largest, to build long-term value among a trusted, delighted tribe, to create work that matters and stands the test of time."
—Seth Godin

149. "A revolution is the ability to take a concept in a new direction that was never contemplated before and rally a group of people around that cause, and see how it benefits the world."
—Unknown

150. "A revolution starts with a clear vision of a world different than the one we live in today."
—Simon Sinek

151.
"We are here to make good things happen for other people."

UNKNOWN

152. "Your primary customer is whoever you communicate with and who depends on you the most."
—Unknown

153. "There is a myth that people who are more successful end up with higher self-esteem. It is totally the opposite, people with higher self-esteem become more successful."
—John R. DiJulius III

154. "A revolution is the ability to rally a group of people around a cause, who are so committed to seeing it through because it will benefit and change the world."
—Unknown

155. "Empathy is an intimate connection with the customer—knowing how they feel."
—John R. DiJulius III

156. "To really win customer loyalty, just be brilliant at the basics."
—John R. DiJulius III

157. "You need to show that you genuinely care about people first, that you realize they are a person with a life and are not just the next customer you are transacting with."
—John R. DiJulius III

158. "Change the term 'customer transactions' to 'customer interactions.'"
—John R. DiJulius III

159. "Today the only way a company can differentiate itself is through building relationships with people, employees, customers, and the community. It is a new era, and people are starving for relationships like never before."
—John R. DiJulius III

160. "Ask yourself two questions: What if we train our staff and they leave? What if we don't train our staff and they stay?"

—Unknown

161. "Use the term 'guidelines' instead of 'policy.' Policy is black and white and it distorts employee creativity. Employees will use it as a crutch and be fearful to ever go against a policy."

—John R. DiJulius III

162. "Give the customer more than they want, and you will end with more than you had hoped."

—John R. DiJulius III

163. "The companies that are flourishing are animated by the purpose motive. The kind of thing that might get you up in the morning and racing to go to work. I think if we can be purpose maximizers, not only profit maximizers, we can actually build organizations and work lives that make us better off and that make our world a little better."
—Daniel Pink

164. "Make a total stranger's day today."
—Brian Shipman

165. "Your smile is your logo, your personality is your business card. How you leave others feeling after having an experience with you becomes your trademark."
—Jerome "Jay" Danzie

166. "Employee apathy creates customer apathy. Nothing will kill a business faster than customer apathy."
—John R. DiJulius III

167.

"Purpose is
the new currency."

JOHN DAME

168. "Nothing can ruin a company's customer experience faster than rapid growth."
—John R. DiJulius III

169. "Show me you know me."
—Four Seasons Hotels

170. "Make a customer, not a sale."
—Katherine Barchetti

171. "When the customer comes first, the customer will last."
—Robert Half International

172. "Your company cannot give good customer service if your employees don't feel good about coming to work."
—Martin Oliver

173. "Service, in short, is not what you do, but who you are. It is a way of living that you need to bring to everything you do if you are to bring it to your customer interactions."
—Betsy Sanders

174. "Businesses need to put the 'customer' back into customer service."
—Unknown

175. "Customers are willing to exchange money for energy. The better the energy, the better the money."
—John R. DiJulius III

176. "It must thrive inside to be experienced outside."
—Joseph Michelli

177. "Your biggest expense is dissatisfied customers."
—John R. DiJulius III

178. "Great brands always make an emotional connection with the intended audience. They reach beyond the purely rational and purely economic level to spark feelings of closeness, affection, and trust. Consumers live in an emotional world; their emotions influence their decisions. Great brands transcend specific product features and benefits and penetrate people's emotions."
—Leonard Berry

179.
"Discounting your prices is just a race to the bottom."

UNKNOWN

180. "Most people come to work for a company having had previous work experiences. In many cases, their experience has been bad. As such, they enter with cynicism, and the burden of proof is on leaders to demonstrate that this is a different place."
—Howard Schultz

181. "We take the ordinary and give it new life . . . believing that what we create has the potential to touch others' lives."
—Howard Schultz

182. "Given the choice, most customers seek out experiences and products that deliver more value, more connection, and more experience, that change us for the better."
—Seth Godin

183. "What it takes to build a world-class, online experience is no different than face-to-face or over the phone."
—John R. DiJulius III

184. "When paying a premium price, the first thing a customer will ask is, 'What was the R.O.X. (Return on eXperience)?'"
—John R. DiJulius III

185. "If a company can consistently meet customers' expectations, that in itself will exceed their expectations."
—Unknown

186. "The best salespeople are the ones who put themselves in their customers' shoes and provide a solution that makes the customer happy."
—Mark Cuban

187. "The best salesperson is the one the customer trusts and never has to question."
—Mark Cuban

188. "The best salesperson is the one who takes immense satisfaction from the satisfaction her customer gets."
—Mark Cuban

189. "You are not the one that determines when it is time to grow. If you are truly great, your customers will demand you get bigger."
—John R. DiJulius III

190. "Love is the most powerful drug. Some people call it passion, purpose, or a calling. However, there is only one common denominator that changes a person to the point where s/he can't wait for the sun to rise, jumping out of bed in the morning, excited about the day. That emotion is 'love,' whether it's romance, your children, hobby, a cause, product, your customer, or career."
—John R. DiJulius III

191. "Love is obsession. Love is adrenaline that will drive you, make you deaf to the naysayers, make you only see the opportunity, and give you the perseverance to withstand the rugged descent when others would bail. Without love, it will be something temporary that eventually gets old. No one has ever accomplished greatness without love."
—John R. DiJulius III

192. "If you fear special requests, if you have to put it all in a manual, then the chances of amazing someone are really quite low."
—Seth Godin

193. "The goal as a company is to have customer service that is not just the best, but legendary."
—Sam Walton

194.
"It's easier to love a brand when the brand loves you back."

SETH GODIN

195. "When people call our call center, our reps don't have scripts, and they don't try to upsell. They are just judged on whether they go above and beyond for the customer and really deliver a kind of personal service and emotional connection with our customers."
—Tony Hsieh

196. "In an era when companies see online support as a way to shield themselves from costly interactions with their customers, it's time to consider an entirely different approach: building human-centric customer service through great people and clever technology. So, get to know your customers. Humanize them. Humanize yourself."
—Kristin Smaby

197. "Don't find fault. Find a remedy."
—Henry Ford

198. "Nothing is so contagious as enthusiasm."
—Edward Bulwer-Lytton

199. "The golden rule, 'Treat people the way you want to be treated,' does not apply to customer service. Employees' previous life and work experiences are typically not how you want them to treat your customers."
—John R. DiJulius III

200. "The way to a customer's heart is much more than a loyalty program. Making customer evangelists is about creating experiences worth talking about."
—Valeria Maltoni

201. "We take most of the money that we could have spent on paid advertising and instead put it back into the customer experience. Then we let the customers be our marketing."
—Tony Hsieh

202. "Repeat business or behavior can be bribed. Loyalty has to be earned."
—Unknown

203. "Get closer than ever to your customers. So close, in fact, that you tell them what they need well before they realize it themselves."
—Steve Jobs

204.
"The customer's perception
is your reality."

KATE ZABRISKIE

205. "Don't find customers for your products; find products for your customers."
—Seth Godin

206. "Revolve your world around the customer, and more customers will revolve around you."
—Unknown

207. "If you make a sale, you make a living. If you make an investment of time and good service in a customer, you can make a fortune."
—Jim Rohn

208. "Recognition is the number one reason why our guests return."
—Danny Meyer

209. "My goal is to make my client a hero."
—John R. DiJulius III

210. "A person's income is not a function of their commission; it is a function of how well they retain clients."
—John R. DiJulius III

211. "Make someone's day today. All it takes is a sincere compliment or display of appreciation."
—John R. DiJulius III

212. "You earn business by being generous with your knowledge and resources without asking for anything in return."
—Unknown

213. "Feeling gratitude and not expressing it is like wrapping a present and not giving it."
—William Arthur Ward

214. "The way you treat your employees is your instruction to them on how to treat customers."
—Shep Hyken

215. "The most powerful and enduring brands are built from the heart. They are real and sustainable. Their foundations are stronger because they are built with the strength of the human spirit, not an ad campaign. The companies that are lasting are those that are authentic."
—Howard Schultz

216. "Things that would have gotten a wow or jazz ten years ago draw a yawn today."
—Steve Wynn

217. "Attitude wins."
—Unknown

218. "Customer experience is the new marketing."
—Unknown

219. "The rules of engagement of traditional marketing, advertising, and public relations is no longer an effective tool because of the way in which people are interacting within the new channels of communications. Now the mistake that most companies are making is they are using these channels as an opportunity to sell stuff. It is really not designed for that. In fact, I would submit that you should really resist that temptation and use social media as a reservoir of trust with your customers."
—Howard Schultz

220. "Always give your competition more credit than you think. Believe they are working harder, thinking out of the box, getting better."
—John R. DiJulius III

221. "I can only trust you if I know you have my back and will stand by me through tough times."
—John R. DiJulius III

222.
"A great partner thinks about their client's success as well as their own."

UNKNOWN

223. "People want to be part of something larger than themselves. They want to be part of something they are proud of, that they'll fight for, sacrifice for, that they trust."
—Howard Schultz

224. "Our strongest competition is our own reputation."
—Unknown

225. "Human experiences are at the heart of your brand."
—Howard Schultz

226. "People can copy your products and your services, but seldom can they build the powerful connections with customers that emerge from the well-designed experiences that you deliver."
—Joseph Michelli

227. "Customer service is not a department. It's a philosophy to be embraced by every person in an organization, from the CEO to the most recently hired. It's everyone's responsibility."
—Shep Hyken

228. "Service is taking action to create value for someone else."
—Ron Kaufman

229. "The best salesperson is the one who knows that with every cold call made, he is closer to helping someone."
—Mark Cuban

230. "We must show people we care instead of trying to manipulate them into buying our product or service."
—John R. DiJulius III

231. "Did you raise the service aptitude of your team today? Did you inspire them by telling what they could do for a customer or maybe by the way you treated an employee or customer?"
—John R. DiJulius III

232. "You can have a great product, but it takes world-class service to create brand loyalty."
—John R. DiJulius III

233.
"Haters aren't your problem; ignoring them is."

JAY BAER

234. "If your existing customers aren't sending new customers to you, you're doing it wrong."
—Joe Calloway

235. "It is a major mistake to allow cheap imitators to appear as your competition by playing into their hands and reducing your prices. You are giving them credibility and decreasing your status as the leader of your industry. If you feel your products and services are superior, then your fees should reflect that. Everyone expects to pay more when they are dealing with the best."
—John R. DiJulius III

236. "When the best is similar in price to rest of the pack, customers get suspicious, and the perception of excellence disappears."
—Unknown

237. "Technology is 10% of the experience, and you are 90%."
—Unknown

238. "When you hire someone, that is the time when you go to work for them."
—Unknown

239. "Recognize everyone, regardless of their position or title; ask for their input and opinions. You may be surprised what you will learn."
—John R. DiJulius III

240. "The majority of customer challenges can be resolved if we simply express sincerely our apology and thank them for giving us the opportunity to correct it."
—John R. DiJulius III

241. "The best marketing is happy team members."
—John R. DiJulius III

242. "We are setting the standard for our competition."
—Unknown

243. "The real scorecard is the number of people's lives you have enhanced."
—John R. DiJulius III

244. "We make a living by what we get, but we make a life by what we give."
—Reuben K. Youngdahl (*Living God's Way*, T.S. Denison, 1953.)

245. "If you're not adding value to others, you are a thief."
—Unknown

246. "We do not remember days, we remember moments."
—Cesare Pavese

247. "As long as you have an idea that improves someone's life or moves society forward, then you have a story to tell. It's up to you to communicate your story in a way that inspires, energizes, and excites your audience."
—Carmine Gallo

248. "I want to live an extraordinary life so countless others will."
—John R. DiJulius III

249. "We don't put employees in John Robert's Spa, we put John Robert's Spa in our employees."
—John R. DiJulius III

250.
"Some people aren't used to an environment where excellence is expected."

STEVE JOBS

251. "You should never start a company with the goal of getting rich. Your goal should be making something you believe in, that will improve people's lives, customers, employees, and the community."
—Steve Jobs

252. "There is no point going anywhere that people don't remember you were there."
—Patricia Fripp

253. "What got you here won't get you there."
—Marshall Goldsmith

254. "Will you be the disruptive force of change?"
—Josh Linkner

255. "If you want happy employees, hire happy people."
—Unknown

256. "Be a day maker; the day maker always benefits the most."
—John R. DiJulius III

257. "Be world class; it is the least crowded."
—John R. DiJulius III

258. "You were meant to change the world, and you were meant to do it today."
—Unknown

259. "If you can't explain it in one sentence, it is not clear enough to you."
—Unknown

260. "To live—the ultimate experience. Always discover and learn. Take risks, fail often, persevere relentlessly, and succeed. Find your passion, your niche. Share and teach. Build amazing relationships, love, feel emotions, be vulnerable, experience loss and joy. Care and show kindness. Constantly appreciate and show gratitude. We must build, innovate, and create opportunity. Always give more and leave things better as a result of your presence."
—John R. DiJulius III

261. "Imagine a world where people wake up every day inspired to go to work, feel safe while they are there, and return home at the end of the day feeling fulfilled by the work they do, feeling that they have contributed to something greater than themselves."
—Simon Sinek

262.

"Expertise is the enemy of innovation."

STEPHEN M. SHAPIRO

263. "A true test of character is how you treat people that can't help you."
—Unknown

264. "There is huge risk in not innovating."
—Unknown

265. "When you look great and feel great, it's easier to do great things."
—Unknown

266. "Don't chase money, chase greatness."
—John R. DiJulius III

267. "The two most important days in your life, the day you are born and the day you find out why."
—Mark Twain

268. "There are three ways you perform: The performance you plan, the one you give, and the one you wish you did."
—Dan Thurmon

269. "Today I shall behave as if this is the day I will be remembered."
—Unknown

270. "Believe in your vision: It gets you out of bed every day. It drives you every day. It is your quest and what gives you meaning in your life. If you don't believe in your vision, no one else ever will. If you're not passionate about your vision, no one else will be either. If you give up on your vision, everyone around you will know it and give up on you."
—Neil Ducoff

271. "The only real measure of success is to count the number of people's lives you added quality to and impacted."
—John R. DiJulius III

272. "We have an obligation to demonstrate gratitude for the life we enjoy."
—Unknown

273. "Everyone is guilty of the good they didn't do."
—Unknown

274. "If your ideas stir up no controversy, arguments, or disbeliefs, then they're not strong enough."
—Unknown

275. "Being interested makes you interesting."
—Unknown

276. "By being the receiver, you are allowing someone else the gift of generosity."
—John R. DiJulius III

277. "Money somehow tracks you down when you're in your place of passion."
—Jack Daly

278. "There will never be a 'perfect time' in your life to do a great thing."
—Unknown

279. "There's only two things you can control: your energy and your attitude."
—John R. DiJulius III

280. "The enemy of implementation is perfection."
—Rob Posner

281. "Greatness is ordinary people producing extraordinary results."
—Jimmy Valvano

282. "If you always do what you have always done, you will always get what you have always gotten."
—Unknown

283.
"You're only limited by your passion and your imagination."

KATHLEEN FLINN

284. "If you want to cheer yourself up, you should try cheering up someone else."
—Unknown

285. "Slogans without actions are lies."
—Unknown

286. "While few may be affluent, all have influence."
—John R. DiJulius III

287. "Sometimes we cannot choose what we do, but we do have a choice in how we do it."
—Unknown

288. "The only difference between ordinary and extraordinary is the little extra."
—Unknown

289. "In order to really win, you must make others around you win first."
—Unknown

290. "No passion = No achievement.
Know passion = Know achievement."
—Unknown

291. "When the goal is to accomplish greatness,
to go where no one or team has gone before,
I am not asking for your best effort; your best
is what you *were* capable of in the past. I am
expecting you to figure it out, try one thousand
ways, if need be try another thousand ways,
innovate, lose sleep, get around it, find loopholes,
research, sweat like you never have before. Every
extraordinary accomplishment, invention, or
revolution was not a result of someone giving his
or her best. Somehow that person or group found
a way to do what no one else could do—they did
the impossible, they did what no one had ever
done before. So the next time you fail, before you
want to make yourself feel better by saying, 'I did
my best,' think about whether you really did."
—John R. DiJulius III

292.

"It took us ten years to be an overnight success."

UNKNOWN

293. "What you permit, you promote."
—Unknown

294. "People are capable of doing amazing things when they have no other choices."
—Unknown

295. "Live it, love it, or leave it."
—Unknown

296. "Every great achievement was once considered impossible."
—Unknown

297. "Success will not lower its standard to us. We must raise our standard to success."
—Randall R. McBride Jr.

298. "Find something you love to do so much, you can't wait for the sun to rise to do it all over again."
—Chris Gardner

299. "Don't sell products, services, or jobs; sell dreams and a vision."
—Unknown

300. "The highest honor I receive is the privilege of helping others achieve their dreams."
—John R. DiJulius III

301. "You have to have a sense of urgency to do what you were born to do, to make an impact, and leave a legacy. Our time is very short, shorter than any of us realize."
—John R. DiJulius III

302. "You don't do something till you can get it right, you do something till you can't get it wrong."
—Unknown

303. "A lot of people are pretty delusional on what it takes to be the best. It is a level of commitment most sane people aren't willing to do."
—Mark Perry

304. "Time is not money; demand is money."
—Van Council

305. "If we don't fail occasionally, we're not taking enough risks."
—Unknown

306. "Nobody rises to low expectations."
—Carl Boyd

307. "It's better to do something for nothing, than nothing for nothing."
—Patricia Fripp

308. "Make a dent in the universe."
—Steve Jobs

309. "Don't embrace the status quo."
—Steve Jobs

310. "Discounting is the tax a business pays for being average."
—John R. DiJulius III

311. "Every product and service eventually gets commoditized. The only thing that doesn't is a memorable experience."
—John R. DiJulius III

312. "Don't forget the 'social' part of social media."
—Unknown

313. "Hugging your haters doesn't mean the customer is right; it means the customer is answered."
—Jay Baer

314.

"Service is to be a present,
engaged presence."

JOHN R. DIJULIUS III

315. "Every interaction you have with another
person (whether customer, employee, friend, or
family member) makes a bigger impact than you
realize. Every single interaction matters. Every
moment makes a difference."

—Donna Cutting

316. "Never lose sight of the impact you make on other people in any given moment. The choice you make to smile (or not), to follow through (or not), to be empathetic (or not) makes a bigger difference than you will ever know."
—Donna Cutting

317. "They focus their energy on making every single guest feel like this time is their time."
—Christina Stratton

318. "We believe that everyone here is up to something great."
—Spencer Forgey

319. "Every time you select someone, your culture gets better or worse."
—Cydney Koukol

320. "If you want to create a consistently positive experience for your customers, then you must hold out for customer service rock stars."
—Donna Cutting

321. "What happens when you hire amazing people is that they are disappointed when they have to work with mediocre people."
—Cydney Koukol

322. "If every employee at your company . . . had to reapply for his or her job annually, how many would you be rehiring?"
—Donna Cutting

323. "Choose the customer over convenience."
—Donna Cutting

324. "Make your employees' time working for your company the most fulfilling, inspiring, and challenging thing they've ever done, so when an opportunity for greatness comes along, they are ready."
—Kendra Neal

325. "Customer service is too important to be left to the customer service department."
—John R. DiJulius III

326. "Build a relationship instead of a sale."
—John R. DiJulius III

327. "Our service aptitude is defined by our life experiences."
—John R. DiJulius III

328. We started by changing a salon and we ended up impacting a community, an industry, people's lives, and affecting the way other companies do business."
—John R. DiJulius III

329. "If you are constantly exceeding your own expectations, maybe you should raise your expectations."
—John R. DiJulius III

330. "If the world doesn't know your name, you haven't done enough."
—Bo DiJulius

331. "Greatness does not choose you, you choose it. Greatness is determined by the choices we make every day, every hour. The ones that are extraordinary choose to be."
—John R. DiJulius III

332. "Living your life to its fullest potential is not an opportunity or a right; it is your responsibility. It is an obligation to be the best version of you possible. Not just for you and how your life will benefit, but for all the people depending on you—your spouse, children, friends, employees, coworkers, customers, and the community."
—John R. DiJulius III

333. "Your undeveloped potential cheats those around you—those you touch, influence, and impact—as well as yourself of joy, satisfaction, and opportunities."
—John R. DiJulius III

334. "What if Martin Luther King, Mother Teresa, Steve Jobs, Bill Gates, Howard Schultz, Walt Disney, Albert Einstein, Abraham Lincoln, Michael Jordan, Oprah Winfrey, The Beatles, or Nelson Mandela chose to be ordinary? What would the world be like today?"
—John R. DiJulius III

335. "I want to be remembered as a great father, family member, friend, and neighbor who happened to be a good business man."
—John R. DiJulius III

336. "A receptionist is like an offensive lineman. The only time their name gets called in a game is when they screwed up. The dozens of times they played their position so well went unnoticed, while everyone else got the recognition."
—John R. DiJulius III

336. "We don't hire people that possess more winning qualities than our competition does; we just find ways to bring out their winning qualities."
—John R. DiJulius III

JOURNAL

....

Ways you can use your journal:

- Use the exercises listed on page 4 with your team members.

- Use it in customer experience meetings.

- Use it as a notepad.

- Create your own customer experience quotes.

- Use it when you are interacting with other businesses, and record ideas of what you enjoy and opportunities that they might have missed in executing a world-class experience.

- Be an experience observer.

....

CREDITS

For permission to reprint copyrighted material, grateful acknowledgment is given to the following sources:

A List Apart (alistapart.com) and Kristin Smaby: From "Being Human Is Good Business" by Kristin Smaby from *A List Apart*, September 6, 2011, accessed February 16, 2016 at http://alistapart.com/article/being-human-is-good-business.

Ron F. Arndt: Quote by Ron F. Arndt from "SATISFYING THE CUSTOMER PAYS $$: SERVICE APTITUDE TEST: COACH RON ARNDT," John DiJulius Customer Experience Blog, 17 Oct. 2012.

Danielle Babb: From *The Accidental Startup* by Danielle Babb. Copyright © 2001 by Danielle Babb. All rights reserved.

Dr. Leonard L. Barry, University Distinguished Professor of Marketing, Mays Business School, Texas A&M University: Quote by Leonard Barry from *Leading the Starbucks Way: 5 Principles for Connecting with Your Customers, Your Products, and Your People* by Joseph A. Michelli.

Chip Bell: From *Customer Loyalty Guaranteed: Create, Lead, and Sustain Remarkable Customer Service*. Copyright © by Chip Bell. All rights reserved.

Meghan Bell on behalf of Stew Leonard: Quote by Stew Leonard.

Bloomberg L.P.: Quote by Jeff Bezos from "Online Extra:

Jeff Bezos on Word-of-Mouth Power" by Robert D. Hof from *Bloomberg Business*, online, August 1, 2004.

Richard Branson: From "Why We Go to Space" by Richard Branson from *Virgin*, January 13, 2015, accessed February 16, 2016 at www.virgin.com/richard-branson/why-we-go-to-space.

Jerry Bruckner: From *The Success Formula For Personal Growth: 2,000 Motivational Quotes, Winning Strategies and Advice from 500 Super Successful People*.

Career Press: From *501 Ways to Roll Out the Red Carpet for Your Customers* by Donna Cutting. Copyright © 2016 by Donna Cutting. Published by Career Press. Wayne, NJ. 800-227-3371. All rights reserved.

Cengage Learning via Copyright Clearance Center: Quote by Martin Oliver from *The Leadership Experience* by Richard L. Daft and Patricia G. Lane. All rights reserved.

CEO Coaching International: Quote by Jack Daly from "The Difference Between a Good Salesperson and a Great One" by Steve Sanduski. Audio blog post. *On Your Mark, Get Set, Grow!* 20 Apr. 2015.

John Dame: From "Purpose Is the New Currency for Businesses and Organizations" by John Dame from *Central Penn Business Journal*, June 12, 2015. accessed online February 17, 2016.

Jerome "Jay" Danzie: "Your SMILE is your LOGO. Your personality is your BUSINESS CARD.How you leave others feeling after having an experience with you becomes your TRADEMARK."

Diversion Books: From *How to Win at the Sport of Business: If I Can Do It, You Can Do It* by Mark Cuban. Copyright © 2011 by Mark Cuban.

Neil Ducoff: "Leading today into tomorrow's unknown" Weblog post. *Monday Morning Wake-Up. Neil Ducoff's No-Compromise Leadership*. 17 March 2014.

F+W Media, Inc.: From *Customer Loyalty Guaranteed* by Chip R. Bell and John R. Patterson. Copyright © 2017 by Chip R. Bell and John R. Patterson. All rights reserved.

Thomas Field: Quote by Thomas Field from "Speaker: Cattle Business All about Chaos" by Mike Ferguson from *Baker City Herald*, online, January 22, 2008.

Kathleen Flinn: From *The Kitchen Counter Cooking School: How a Few Simple Lessons Transformed Nine Culinary Novices into Fearless Home Cooks* by Kathleen Flinn. Copyright © 2011 by Kathleen Flinn. All rights reserved.

Patricia Fripp: From "Thoughts and Quotes from Patricia Fripp" from www.fripp.com/about-patricia-fripp/frippicisms.

Carmine Gallo: From *The Innovation Secrets of Steve Jobs: Insanely Different: Principles for Breakthrough Success* by Carmine Gallo. Copyright © 2011 by Carmine Gallo.

Jeffrey Gitomer: From "Buy Gitomer: Satisfied or Loyal—Which Are Your Customers?—Column Archive." from *Buy Gitomer*, 1999, accessed February 17, 2016, http://gitomer.com/articles/ViewPublicArticle. html?key=ajcdMibak3NhWRr%2BIDy%2Fhw%3D%3D.

The Globe and Mail: From "Confessions of a Concierge" from *The Globe and Mail*, April 15, 2006, http://www.theglobeandmail. com/life/confessionsofaconcierge/article706780/?page=all>.

Goldhirsh Group via CopyrightClearence Center:: From "No. 1 Marketing Mistake You're Making" by James Archer from *Inc.com*, 05 Dec. 2012.

Marshall Goldsmith: Quote by Marshall Goldsmith from www.

marshallgoldsmithlibrary.com/cim/What-Got-You-Here.php.

Hachette Books: From *Pour Your Heart Into It* by Howard Schultz and Dori Jones.

Tony Hseih: Quotes by Tony Hseih.

Interview Magazine: Quote by Eric Phillip Cowell from "Simon Cowell" by Dmitri Ehrlich from *Interview Magazine*. August 25, 2011, accessed February 16, 2016, www.interviewmagazine.com/culture/simoncowell/.

Michael Dalton Johnson: From *Top Dog Sales Secrets: 50 Top Experts Show You Proven Ways to Skyrocket Your Sales* by Michael Dalton Johnson. Published by Penny Union, 2007.

Ron Johnson: Quote by Ron Johnson from *The Apple Experience: The Secrets of Delivering Insanely Great Customer Service* by Carmine Gallo. All rights reserved.

Ron Kaufman: Excerpt from http://ronkaufman.com/media_post/uplifting-your-service/. All rights reserved.

Jack Mackey, CCXP, Vice President, Sales, and Chief Evangelist, Service Management Group (SMG): Quote by Jack Mackey from *What's the Secret? To Providing a World-class Customer Experience* by John R. DiJulius.

David Maister: From "A Matter of Trust." from *Davidmaister.com*, 1998. Accessed February 16, 2016. All rights reserved.

Valeria Maltoni: From "Customer Loyalty Comes from Conversation" by Valeria Maltoni from *Conversation Agent,* www.conversationagent.com/2009/02/customer-loyalty-comes-from-conversation-.html.

Danny Meyer: Excerpt from speech by Danny Meyer. All rights reserved.

Joseph Michelli: Quotes by Joseph Michelli.

Thomas Nelson. www.thomasnelson.com: From *Burn: Live the Compassion of Jesus* by Brian Shipman. Copyright © 2001 by Brian Shipman.

Mark Perry: Quote by Mark Perry.

Portfolio: an imprint of Penguin Publishing Group, a division of Penguin Random House LLC: From *Street Smarts: An All-Purpose Tool Kit for Entrepreneurs* by Norm Brodsky and Bo Burlingham. Copyright © 2008 by Norm Brodsky and Bo Burlingham. From *Best Practices Are Stupid: 40 Ways to Out-Innovate the Competition* by Stephan M. Shapiro. Copyright © 2011 by Stephen M. Shapiro.

Jim Rohn International: From *Jim Rohn, America's Foremost Business Philosopher*. Copyright ©2016. As a world-renowned author and success expert, Jim Rohn touched millions of lives during his forty-six-year career as a motivational speaker and messenger of positive life change. For more information on Jim and his popular personal achievement resources or to subscribe to the weekly Jim Rohn newsletter, visit www.JimRohn.com.

Rotary International: "One Profits Most Who Serves Best" is a trademark of Rotary International.

Brian Shipman: Quote by Brian Shipman. Copyright © by Brian Shipman. All rights reserved.

Simon & Schuster, Inc.: From *Steve Jobs* by Walter Isaacson. Copyright © 2011 by Walter Isaacson. All rights reserved.

Simon Sinek author of bestselling books *Start with Why* and *Leaders Eat Last*: Quote by Simon Sinek. All rights reserved.

Transaction Publishers: From *This Business of Living: Diary: 1935-1950* by Cesar Pavese. All rights reserved.

Tyndale House Publishers, Inc.: Some content taken from *The DNA of Relationships* by Dr. Gary Smalley. Copyright © 2004. All rights reserved.

Wal-mart: Quote by Sam Walton from "A Vision for Leading on Data and Personalization" by Roz Brewer from Walmart Shareholders Meeting 2014, from Walmart.com, accessed February 17, 2016.

Wayne State University Press: From *Young Henry Ford: A Picture History of the First Forty Years* by Sidney Olson. Copyright © 1963 by Wayne State University Press.

John Wiley and Sons: Quote by Sam Walton from *The 10 Rules of Sam Walton: Success Secrets for Remarkable Results* by Michael Bergdahl, Foreword by Rob Walton. Copyright © 2007 by John Wiley and Sons. From *Evolve or Die: Seven Steps to Rethink the Way You Do Business* by Robin Crow. Copyright © 2010 by Robin Crow. All rights reserved. From *How to Persuade and Influence People: Powerful Techniques to Get Your Own Way More Often* by by Philip Hesketh. Copyright © 2010 by Philip Hesketh. From *Warren Buffett Speaks: Wit and Wisdom from the World's Greatest Investor*, 2nd Edition, by Janet Lowe. Copyright © 2007 by John Wiley and Sons. All rights reserved. From *Fabled Service: Ordinary Acts, Extraordinary Outcomes* by Bonnie Jameson and Betsy Sanders. Copyright © 1997 by John Wiley and Sons. All rights reserved. From *Disciplined Dreaming: A Proven System to Drive Breakthrough Creativity* by Josh Linkner. Copyright © 2011 by Josh Linkner. All rights reserved. Quote by Robert Half from *The Reactor Factor: How to Handle Difficult Work Situations Without Going Nuclear* by Marsha Petrie Sue. Copyright © 2009 by John Wiley and Sons. All rights reserved.

Kate Zabriskie: Quote by Kate Zabriskie.

Zig Ziglar: Quote by Zig Ziglar.

ABOUT THE AUTHOR

As *the* authority on world-class customer experience, organizations across the world use John's philosophies and methodology for creating world-class service. He has worked with companies such as the Ritz-Carlton, Lexus, Starbucks, Nordstrom, Panera Bread, Nestlé, Marriott Hotel, PWC, Cheesecake Factory, Progressive Insurance, Harley-Davidson, State Farm, Chick-fil-A, and many more to help them continue to raise the bar and set the standard in service that consistently exceeds customer expectations.

John is the president of The DiJulius Group, a customer service consulting firm whose purpose is to change the world by creating a customer service revolution. He is also the founder and the owner of John Robert's Spa, an upscale chain (with over 150 employees), which has been named one of the Top 20 Salons in America. John resides in Aurora, Ohio, with his three boys, Johnni, Cal, and Bo.

CPSIA information can be obtained
at www.ICGtesting.com
Printed in the USA
LVHW020936250222
711994LV00024B/1394

9 781632 990877